Dear Parent:

Congratulations! Your child is taking
the first steps on an exciting journe
The destination? Independent readi

STEP INTO READING® will help
five steps to reading success. Each s
There are also Step into Reading Sti
Readers, Step into Reading Write-In
Readers, and Step into Reading Pho
literacy program with something for

Learning to Read, Step

Ready to Read   Pre
• big type and easy words • rhyme and rhythm • picture clues
For children who know the alphabet and are eager to
begin reading.

Reading with Help   Preschool–Grade 1
• basic vocabulary • short sentences • simple stories
For children who recognize familiar words and sound out
new words with help.

Reading on Your Own   Grades 1–3
• engaging characters • easy-to-follow plots • popular topics
For children who are ready to read on their own.

Reading Paragraphs   Grades 2–3
• challenging vocabulary • short paragraphs • exciting stories
For newly independent readers who read simple sentences
with confidence.

Ready for Chapters   Grades 2–4
• chapters • longer paragraphs • full-color art
For children who want to take the plunge into chapter books
but still like colorful pictures.

STEP INTO READING® is designed to give every child a successful
reading experience. The grade levels are only guides. Children can progress
through the steps at their own speed, developing confidence in their
reading, no matter what their grade.

Remember, a lifetime love of reading star

D1021801

To Fran Penner

Text copyright © 1995 by Lucille Recht Penner.
Illustrations copyright © 1995 by Jada Rowland.
All rights reserved under International and Pan-American Copyright Conventions.
Published in the United States by Random House Children's Books, a division of Random House,
Inc., New York, and simultaneously in Canada by Random House of Canada Limited, Toronto.

www.stepintoreading.com

Educators and librarians, for a variety of teaching tools, visit us at
www.randomhouse.com/teachers

Library of Congress Cataloging-in-Publication Data
Penner, Lucille Recht.
The Statue of Liberty / by Lucille Recht Penner ; illustrated by Jada Rowland.
  p. cm. — (Step into reading. A step 2 book)
Previously published: 1996.
SUMMARY: Relates the construction of the Statue of Liberty and its importance as a
symbol of freedom.
ISBN 0-679-86928-X (trade) — ISBN 0-679-96928-4 (lib. bdg.)
1. Statue of Liberty (New York, N.Y.)—Juvenile literature. 2. New York (N.Y.)—Buildings,
structures, etc.—Juvenile literature. [1. Statue of Liberty (New York, N.Y.)
2. New York (N.Y.)—Buildings, structures, etc.]
I. Rowland, Jada, ill. II. Title. III. Series: Step into reading. Step 2 book.
F128.64.L6 P48 2003 974.7'1—dc21 2002015109

Printed in the United States of America
23 22 21 20

STEP INTO READING, RANDOM HOUSE, and the Random
House colophon are registered trademarks of
Random House, Inc.

The Statue of Liberty

by Lucille Recht Penner

illustrated by Jada Rowland

Random House 🏠 New York

A lady stands in

New York Harbor.

She is as tall as a

skyscraper.

She is called

the Statue of Liberty.

"Liberty" means freedom.
All over the world,
people dreamed
of coming to America
to find freedom.

People came by ship.

The trip took many days.

Men, women, and children
were crowded together.

They were tired, hungry,
and scared.

Suddenly they saw the lady!
They had reached
America at last.
Now they knew
they were free.
People cried for joy.

The Statue of Liberty
was a present
from the people of France
to the people of the
United States.

A Frenchman made the lady.

His name was

Frédéric Bartholdi.

He copied his mother's face

for his statue.

How beautiful she was!

First Frédéric made
a small statue.

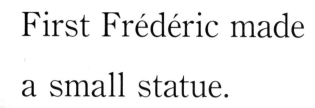

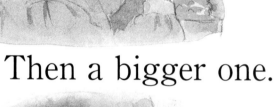

Then a bigger one.

Then an even
bigger one.

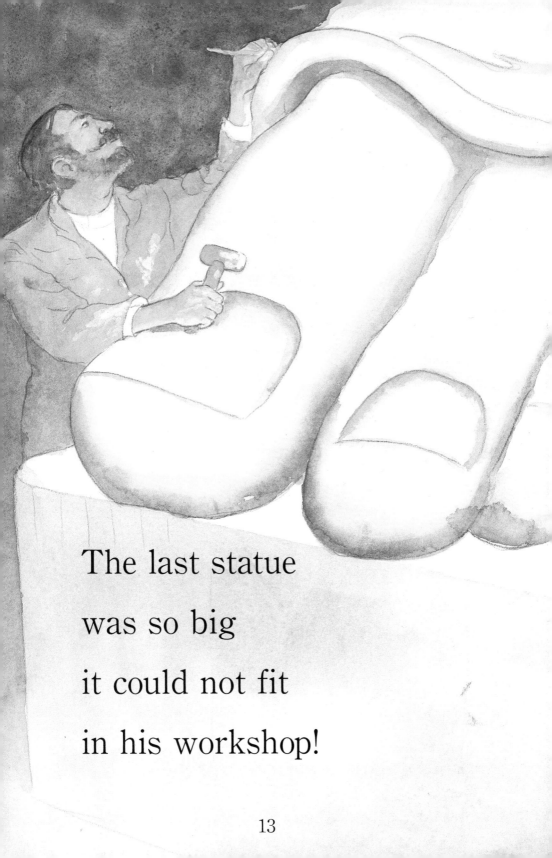

The last statue
was so big
it could not fit
in his workshop!

He had to make it

in pieces.

He made the right hand

holding the torch.

Then he made

the head.

Each finger was longer
than a man.
Each eye was as big
as a child.

Frédéric needed
lots of help.
His helpers worked
in a big room.

They took
the pieces outside
and put them together.
She was higher than
all the buildings.
Much higher!

Workers took
the statue apart.
They packed it
in 214 crates.

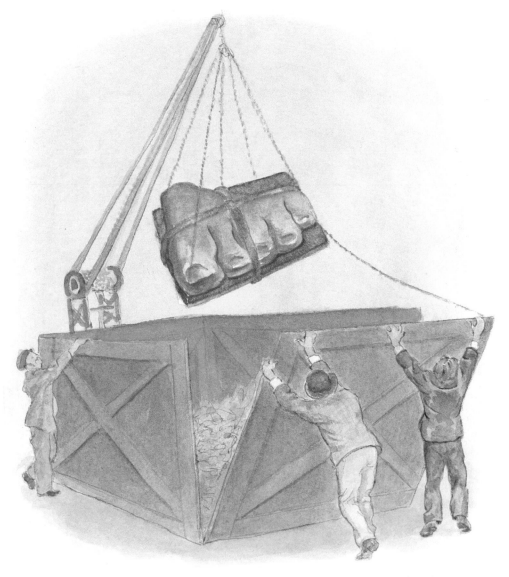

A ship carried it
from France to New York.

In America
the people
were building
a high pedestal
for the lady to stand on.

But they ran
out of money!
The work stopped.
No one knew
what to do.

Joseph Pulitzer owned

a newspaper.

He had an idea.

Joseph said, "The statue
needs a home!
I will print the name
of everyone who gives
money to help."
Thousands of people
sent nickels and dimes.
Children sent pennies.
Soon there was
enough money.

Now workers could finish
the huge pedestal.
They set the lady
on top of it.

A big French flag

was draped over her face.

On October 28, 1886,
the people of New York
had a parade
to welcome her.

The President of
the United States
made a speech.
Frédéric Bartholdi
was excited!
He raced up a staircase
inside the statue.
Up and up he went
to the very top.

Frédéric looked down.
A boy was waving
a white handkerchief.
It was the signal.
Frédéric pulled a rope
and the flag fell.

There was the lady!

Hip, hip, hurrah!

Cannons boomed.

Boat whistles blew.

People cheered.

The excitement
never ended.
Today, more than
one hundred years later,
the Statue of Liberty
still welcomes people
to America—
the land of the free.